piano · vocal · guitar

best of
JUDY COLLINS

ISBN-13: 978-1-4234-5313-0
ISBN-10: 1-4234-5313-1

HAL•LEONARD®
CORPORATION

7777 W. BLUEMOUND RD. P.O. BOX 13819 MILWAUKEE, WI 53213

Visit Hal Leonard Online at
www.halleonard.com

ALBATROSS

Words and Music by
JUDY COLLINS

Moderately, brooding and melancholy

1. The la-dy comes to the
2. *(See additional lyrics)*

gate.

Dressed in lav-en-der and leath-er

look-ing North to the sea she finds the weath-er fine,

she hears the stee-ple bells _____ ring-ing through the or-chard

all the way from town. She watch-es sea-gulls

fly sil-ver on the o-cean stitch-ing through the waves the edg-es of the

Additional Lyrics

2. Even now by the gate
   With your long hair blowing,
   And the colors of the day
   That lie along your arms,
   You must barter your life
   To make sure you are living,
   You give them the colors,
   And the bells and wind and the dreams.
   Will there never be a prince
   Who rides along the sea and the mountains,
   Scattering the sand and foam
   Into amethyst fountains,
   Riding up the hills from the beach
   In the long summer grass,
   Holding the sun in his hands
   And shattering the isinglass?
   Day and night and day again,
   And people come and go away forever,
   While you search the waves for love
   And your visions for a sign,
   The knot of tears around your throat
   Is crystalizing into your design...

   Chorus
   And in the night the iron wheels
   Rolling through the rain
   Down the hills through the long grass
   To the sea,
   And in the dark the hard bells
   Ringing with pain,
   Come away alone...
   Come away alone...with me.

AMAZING GRACE

Traditional
Arranged by JUDY COLLINS

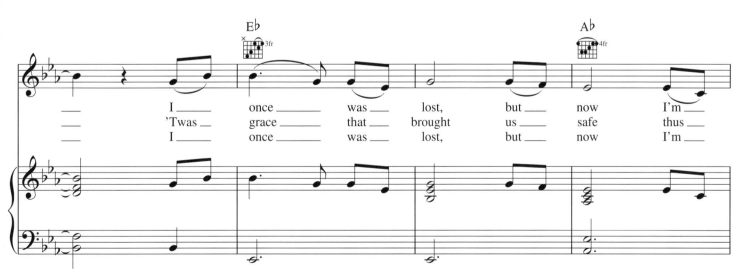

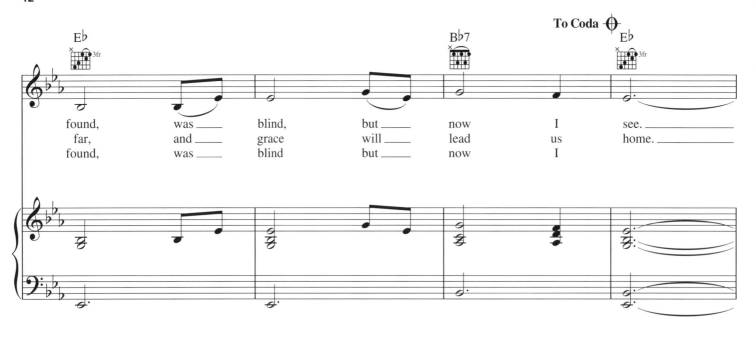

found,   was ___ blind,   but ___ now   I   see. ___
far,   and ___ grace   will ___ lead   us   home. ___
found,   was ___ blind   but ___ now   I

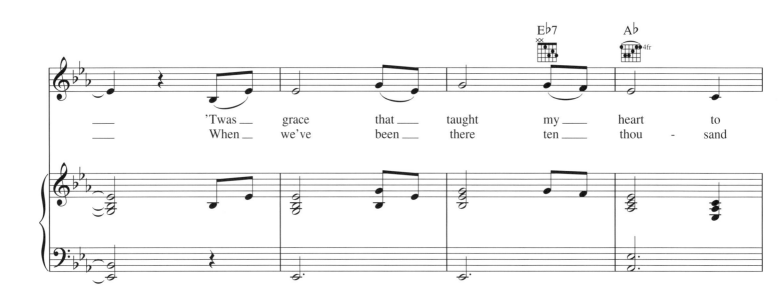

___ 'Twas ___ grace that ___ taught my ___ heart to
___ When ___ we've been ___ there ten ___ thou - sand

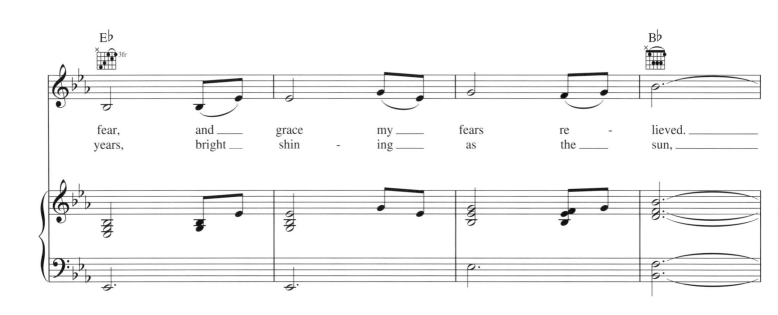

fear,   and ___ grace my ___ fears   re -   lieved. ___
years,   bright ___ shin - ing ___ as   the ___ sun, ___

BORN TO THE BREED

Words and Music by
JUDY COLLINS

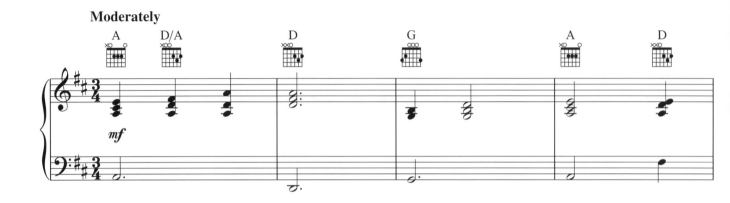

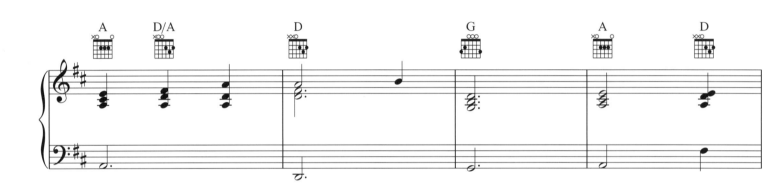

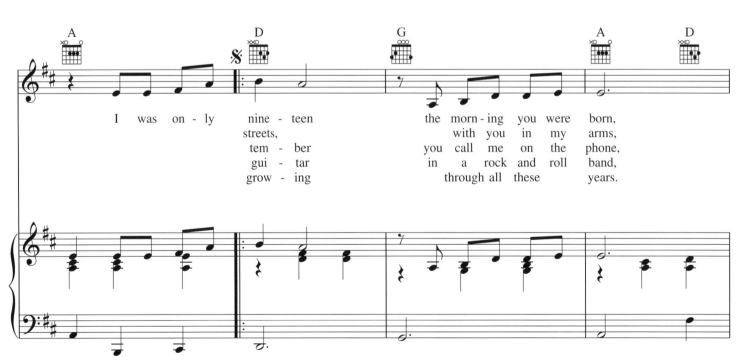

I was on - ly nine - teen   the morn - ing you were born,
streets,   with you in my arms,
tem - ber   you call me on the phone,
gui - tar   in a rock and roll band,
grow - ing   through all these years.

BOTH SIDES NOW

Words and Music by
JONI MITCHELL

MY FATHER

Words and Music by
JUDY COLLINS

Lyrically, nostalgic

(1.) My (4.) fa - ther al - ways prom-ised us _____ that
(2.) All my sis - ters soon were gone _____ to
(3.) And I live in Par - is now, _____ my

we _____ would live _____ in France, we'd go boat - ing
Den - ver and _____ Chey-enne; mar - ry - ing their
chil - dren dance _____ and dream. Hearing the ways of

on the Seine _____ and I would learn to dance.
grown-up dreams, _____ the li - lac and the man.
a min-er's life, in worlds they've nev - er seen.

SEND IN THE CLOWNS

from the Musical A LITTLE NIGHT MUSIC

Music and Lyrics by
STEPHEN SONDHEIM

Moderately slow, freely

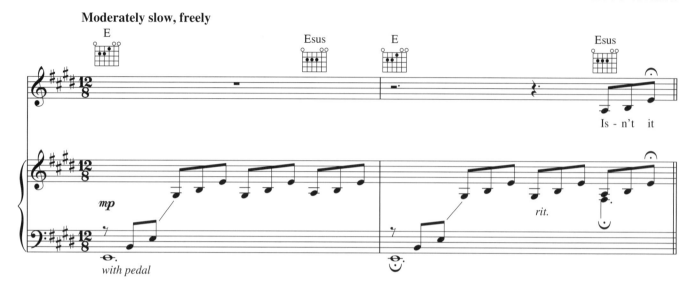

Is - n't it

rich?
bliss?
Are we a pair?
Don't you ap - prove?
Me here at
One who keeps

last on the ground, you in mid - air...
tear - ing a - round, one who can't move...
Send in the
Where are the

SO EARLY, EARLY IN THE SPRING

Traditional
Arranged by JUDY COLLINS

SINCE YOU'VE ASKED

Words and Music by
JUDY COLLINS

SONG FOR JUDITH
(Open the Door)

Words and Music by
JUDY COLLINS

SUZANNE

Words and Music by
LEONARD COHEN

Madrigal mode

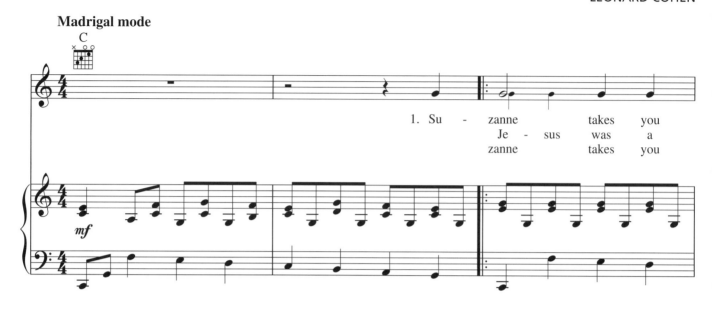

1. Su - zanne takes you
Je - sus was a
zanne takes you

down _____ to her place by the riv - er. You can
sail - or when He walked up - on the wa - ter. And He
down _____ to her place by the riv - er. You can

hear the boats go by, _____ you can spend the night for -
spent a long time watch - ing from a lone - ly wood - en
hear the boats go by, _____ you can spend the night for -

TURN! TURN! TURN!
(To Everything There Is a Season)

Words from the Book of Ecclesiastes
Adaptation and Music by PETE SEEGER

Moderately

To ev-'ry-thing (turn, turn, turn) there is a sea-son (turn, turn, turn) and a time for ev-'ry pur-pose un-der heav-en.

To Coda

WHO KNOWS WHERE THE TIME GOES

Words and Music by
SANDY DENNY

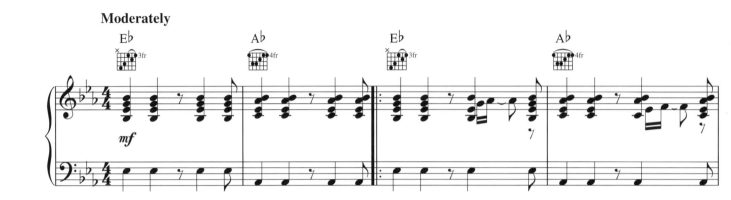

A-cross the morn-ing sky
Sad de-sert-ed shore
And I'm not go - ing

all the birds are leav -
your fick-le friends are _____ leav -
while my love is near _____

ing.
ing,
me.

Ah, _____ how can they know it's time for
ah, _____ but then you know it's time for
And _____ I know it will be so, 'til it's